STAY

Your life is precious

1/19/24;
added to
book list

IMAOBONG SMART

DISCLAIMER

This book is not a medical or psychiatric point of view and does not offer any medical or psychiatric advice.

It represents the sole view of the author and publisher and is intended for information purposes only, reader's discretion is advised

TO MY READERS

Dear friend, thank you for choosing this book to read, you had other options, but you chose this one. you are highly appreciated.

My intentions as I wrote this book was simply to talk to you the way I would, if I saw you on the edge of a cliff about to take that jump, not just that, but also to equip you with inspiring words to say to someone you know who is about to throw in the towel on life. This is from one human to another.

In my husband's words; this book is short, sharp and loaded with inspiring nuggets.

Best wishes,

Imaobong Smart

DEDICATION

This book is dedicated first to God, my Dad, for inspiring me to write this book and to all those who are struggling with depression and suicidal thoughts.

CONTENTS

THE SAD STAT

According to the world health organization, close to 800,000 people die to suicide every year; that is one person every 40 seconds.

According to the center for disease control and prevention, suicide was the tenth leading cause of death in the United States, the second leading cause of death among people aged 10-34 and the fourth leading cause of death for people aged 35-54. There were more than twice as many suicides in the United States as there were homicides.

In 2017, 10.6 million adults 18 and older reported having suicidal thoughts and trying to kill themselves. 1.4 million adults made non-fatal suicidal attempts amongst those who attempted suicide, 1.2 million of them reported making suicidal plans.

Don't be among the heart-breaking statistic.

Toll-free suicide hotline 18002738255 or text HOME to 741741.

12/5/23

INTRODUCTION

Somewhere in the continent of Africa, West Africa to be precise in a country called Nigeria, a young man who was unhappy with his life decided that the day had come for him to end it all. Sam was only 35 years of age and had accomplished nothing in his life; he had dropped out of high school because life was hard at home and he could not keep his focus. He got a job at a local gas station and shared an apartment with his friend Tayo. Sam spent his free time obsessing over the lives of celebrities who were in his age range or younger than himself, wondering why his life couldn't be like theirs, he cursed his family and wondered why he was not born into a wealthy one, he despised his childhood because it was filled with horrible memories, absent and abusive father and a loving mother who was too busy because she had to work several jobs to put food on the table but died of a terrible disease when he was 19. He wondered why he did not have any talents at all, or so he thought.

One day, his only friend and roommate decided to move to another city as he had gotten a new job and left Sam alone to foot the tiny apartment's bill, but Sam could not keep up. So, the next month, he was evicted and on the streets with nowhere to go!

One morning, he woke up where he had laid beside the house of a stranger with such a heavy depression and decided to take a walk in the forest by the mountain of the village called Eyop. He mumbled to himself about how miserable his life was and raised his fist at God for giving him such ill-luck in life and decided "It's over, I'm done, nobody will miss me I will do it, I need rest from this useless life."

He began to climb the mountain, his leg slipped in the middle of his climb, but he managed to gain his balance and kept on going. Finally, he got to the top, and it was about 100 feet tall. He looked down, and the sight invoked some goosebumps out of him then, he began to cry as he took baby steps towards the edge, suddenly, he stopped crying because of a sound he heard.

He thought it was voices from the underworld. He pinched his hands to be sure he was still alive, maybe he could now hear the voices of the spirits because he was about to join them but, the sound was too real, so he slowly backed away from the edge of the mountain looked around and spotted a young woman who was crying loud "Why me God! what did I ever do to deserve this? I hate my life! There is nothing to live for."

He took a closer look at her; she was a few feet away from him on the other side of the mountain, she looked weird at first but then, he realized she was pregnant. He called out to her, "Hey, pregnant lady! Don't do it, whatever it is you are about to do, don't do it yet, wait for me." The woman, surprised that anyone was on the mountain, backed away from the edge, and sat on the ground sobbing terribly. Sam asked her, "Are you trying to kill yourself?" She nodded yes, so he sat close to her and tried to share in her sorrow, and she began to tell him her story.

"My name is Nosa. I am 6 months pregnant, and I am 15. I was forced to get married to my boyfriend who is now my husband. I planned to marry him, but not until I was done with my university, at least, that was our plan, but my father is an elder in the community, and my mistake was going to cost him his pride and respect from the people. My boyfriend who is now my husband was not ready to marry me. In fact, he suddenly detested me after he heard of my pregnancy and accused me of preventing his uncle from sponsoring him into the university because he got me pregnant and demanded that I abort the baby, but I could not.

So, we got married. It was the worst day of both our lives but especially mine. He was only 19 at the time, but he had started drinking and being wild, he would come home every night and beat me up so badly, but two nights ago I became certain that this life is not meant for me to live; it is worthless and cruel. I won't miss not being in this world, and it sure won't miss me and, I am not about to bring a child into this filthy world!

My so-called husband, the boy that once cherished me, came home with three of his drunk friends, and they raped me. I begged them if not for my life but for the baby, but each of them had their turn with me until I passed out. I woke up all alone; my husband's belongings were gone! I have no way of reaching him. Why didn't he just leave without destroying my life!" She continued to wail bitterly.

At this point, Sam began to convince and encourage her that the best way to pay life back would be to stand strong against all odds. He told her that she deserved life, and nothing or no one had the power to determine when her life begins or ends. He encouraged her to cry out as much as she could while he held her in his arms and they sat together crying for hours and for a moment when she was quiet, Sam said to her "A few hours ago, I would have thought that my situation was the worse one on the planet. I was here to take my own life but look at me, helping someone else STAY alive." God has just healed me from my own pain.

Running away from our problems seems to be the easiest way to escape them but, the truth is, what we refuse to handle, fight against, and end NOW will eventually end us!

According to the center for diseases control, suicide is on its high right now than ever before. But why? Is there a depression virus on the loose?

As a matter of fact, despite years of research as it pertains to clinical depression, scientists at the US National Institute of Mental Health and research universities around the world are unsure about the cause of depression.

So, allow me to reason on a rational everyday human being level with you. I don't want to address you on a scientific level because I am not one. I simply want to talk to you the way I would if I saw that knife against your wrist, and we both had no phones! This is straight from the heart.

DEPRESSION TRIGGERS

We live in a fallen world where bad things happen, even to babies. We live in a society where we want everything to happen in our lives in lightning speed time, we are rigid in our plans and expectations and, we leave no room for disappointments, interruptions, and delays. If things don't happen the way we envisioned, we grow impatient, worry and get depressed about how things have not turned out the way we hoped they would.

Depression is caused by things that we have experienced in life that we assume we cannot handle. Nobody just wakes up and has depression. Often there are battles they are fighting silently without any horizontal or vertical help, and it begins to hurt them. It gets stronger if not addressed soon enough.

Depression, which increases suicidal thoughts is caused by our emotions, feelings of hatred, unforgiveness, fear, failure, anger, impatience, confusion, loneliness, anxiety, hurt and guilt. These are the things that cause heaviness in our hearts. Nobody is born with a depression gene. When life happens, and we mishandle that happening in our lives, it leads to all these emotions that bring about depression, which triggers suicidal thoughts. Truth is, we all have been victims of these emotions. I have experienced depression in some forms, postpartum depression, depression because of financial lack and the feeling of being stuck in life.

Someone very close to me experienced depression because of the guilt of something she had done; she didn't want to get out of bed for any reason. She would get angry for waking up in the morning and was mad at everyone for no justifiable reason, and soon enough, she began cutting her wrist with a razor to practice how she would do it for real. One day, she called me and said her "final" goodbye, but I was able to talk her out of it, and today she is enjoying life. The same things I said that helped her through her dark times, is the exact same thing and more that I will share with you in this book. I hope that as you read this book, a new sense of hope will flood your heart!

The purpose of this book is to expose the delusion of suicide and debunk the myths that we try to hold on to in other to justify the act.

I hope that this book will encourage millions of people in the world to overcome depression and suicidal thoughts and save the lives of future world changers. You are the wonder that the world is waiting for. Please stay alive for us! Please STAY here.

"Anxiety leads to depression, but a good word encourages"
– King Solomon

Here are my kind words, I hope it encourages you.

THE LIES YOU BELIEVE AND THE TRUTH YOU MUST ACCEPT

1

The lie you believe

"So many bad things are happening to me, it's a sign that the universe doesn't want me."

"In this world, you will have troubles but, take heart, I have overcome the world"- Jesus

I was getting ready for school when I was 21 when my father started to get sick. At that time, my mother was not working because my father didn't want her to, although she was an attorney. So, my father was entirely responsible for all the finances at home. When he got sick, we all thought it was minor, that it was going to go away. But early one morning, just two days from when he fell ill, my grandma had gone to check on him, and he was cold on his bed. He died in his sleep.

My world was shattered! How was I going to go to school, how was I going to help my two younger siblings? We were not street smart. We totally relied on the provision of our father, and now he was dead! Where I come from, there is a level of stigma attached to fatherless children, and society, especially family members take advantage of that. Things got harder and harder, but somehow, my mother managed to send me to school, and I was glad to be leaving the house.

When I was in my third year in school, leaving me with one year to graduate with my bachelors in biochemistry, my grades were so poor that I was asked to leave school. I couldn't tell my mother, not just for the shame of it but for the fact that at that time she was sick. A few months after her illness she died. This was an incredibly depressing time for me. I lost both parents four years apart! I was barely recovering from the first tragedy when the second one struck!

After the death of my mother and me wasting three years of my life in school all for nothing, I decided to relocate to the United States. At that time, my siblings and I had no one to call family but us because my parents were not in good terms with pretty much the whole of their family. A lot of their siblings did not even show up for their funeral; that's how bad it was. But there was this aunt of ours, her name was Ofonime. She was my mother's younger sister and the only one that we could relate with. She was the consolation we had that although our parents had both passed away 4 years apart, we had someone who loved us and truly cared for us.

Four years later, just after getting married, Ofonime had traveled to another state in Nigeria to celebrate her birthday with her in-laws, but on her way back to her state, the flight she boarded crashed! She died! I will never forget that day. She boarded Dana Air, flight 992, June 3rd, 2012. As I write this, I am yet to recover from her death. I was furious. I questioned God; I wanted to know why He would take away everything important to me and for the second time I truly felt like an orphan! I went through another moment of depression. I didn't want to speak to anyone or go anywhere. I felt so heavy in my heart, I kept having reoccurring nightmares about the crash, I had nights where I couldn't sleep, I would simply cry and cry some more! It seems like the previous two losses happened again in the last one! I was deeply wounded and sorrowful but, I had something that did not allow the overwhelming feeling of depression engulf me, and that was my relationship with my husband and God.

Bad things happen to everyone on the planet, no matter how old or young. No matter your status in life, as long as we live in this fallen world, we will always be victims of bad things. But that doesn't mean that it is a sign to deprive us of our amazing and precious life. "Bad things" is a part of life; it just is, and it is not your fault. That's just the world we live in. But, look at it from a different angle with me for a second.

Imagine for a second that diamonds could talk. What do you think that shiny stone that people kill and die for will tell you about pain, pressure, and heat? Life's challenges and events are not to force you to take your precious life, but to bring out the diamond in you, the chiseling, the burning, the pressure, the scrubbing, the back to back failures, can make you strong if you allow it. The best way to look at this is to understand that life is not always about you, that what happens to you is not always personal. When you scale through this motion (I believe you will), your success story can be the bridge for someone who is going to go through their own depression to cross over to their own success in overcoming depression and suicidal thoughts. The universe wants you—more than you can imagine. Your presence on this earth is very much needed.

The truth you must accept

"Bad things may happen to me, but it won't last forever."

I know you think that when you commit suicide that it's all about you, that no one is getting hurt, that you are simply removing one more miserable life from the earth, that it is fewer tears to wet another's shoulder, it's one less problem in the world but, truth is, it is one more solution removed from the world, it's another blessing taken away from us, it's another miracle that we will never experience, another song we will never hear, another book we will never read, another work of art we will never gaze upon. Suicide is not just the death of you, but the death of many whose lives and destinies depend on you.

MARTIN LUTHER KING JR.

Throughout American history, only four people have ever been honored with a national holiday. Martin Luther King, Jr. is one of them, but when he was twelve, he tried to jump through the second-story window of his home because he was guilt-ridden as a result of his absence when his grandmother died. Think for a moment: what the world, especially for the African Americans, would have been like without a Martin Luther giving us the gift of his existence? You cannot afford to live your life never thinking beyond your present circumstances. You can be great and, one day, you will share your survival story and help someone else who may be in a similar situation you are today.

Some of the best ideas come out of us under extreme pressures when it looks as if all the elements of the universe have had a meeting to torture us out of this earth. Your pain is a miracle in disguise.

WHY BAD THINGS HAPPEN

Because of your own mistakes: We all have had our share of mistakes in our lives and, depending on the severity of the mistakes, it could trigger other series of negative happenings around us or not. Some learn faster from their mistakes, but for some, it takes them a few more mistakes to finally learn and, the more time it takes for them to learn from their mistakes, the more negative consequences they incur on themselves.

We are responsible for our actions, and for the most part, we cannot hide from the consequences that come with it, but there are ways to deal with ourselves when we have made mistakes.

- Accept that you made a mistake

- Remember, everyone makes mistakes

- Know why you made that mistake (Be honest with yourself and don't blame anyone). Was it because you had no mentors, you did not do enough research, you gave in to a deadly lustful experience, you were not ready when your opportunity came, or you allowed yourself to be talked into what you did?

- Find ways to cope with the consequences in a healthy manner, talk to someone you trust and believe in, go for counseling, write your feelings down in a journal to let out your frustration, forgive yourself, encourage yourself!

- Learn from the mistakes and find ways to avoid them, know what it was you did or didn't do that led to the mistakes, what kind of friends do you hang around, who do you need to cut out of your life?

- Don't drown yourself in the thoughts of the mistakes. There are no time machines, stop replaying in your head how you should have avoided it. Move on from it, the future is bright.

Because of someone's wrongdoing: A very close family member of mine was sexually molested at the age of four by an uncle. She was also raped at the age of nineteen by someone she trusted. She struggled with depression as a result of that experience for a few years, but with help from her family and her church, she found the courage to live beyond her bad experiences, and this has not marred her ability to have a healthy male romantic relationship. She decided not to allow her bad experience to dictate the rest of her beautiful life that lies ahead of her.

On the other hand, there is another victim who was sexually molested at the age of nine by a close family friend. She told her family, but no one believed her; this got her enraged, and she struck out on her own at the age of 13 and started living a wildlife, and ended up in jail several times. She also attempted suicide on various occasions. She did not have a way of coping with the wrong that was done to her especially from her family, for not believing her and investigating the matter but now, through counseling and through her church, she has given up that lifestyle and is working on ways to overcome her hurt and focus on her future. There are ways to deal with yourself when you have been wronged.

- It is not your fault. Whoever wronged you made a choice to do so, and just as you are responsible for your reactions to someone's actions, so also are they! You are not to blame!

- Forgive them. Please don't roll your eyes on this one, think for a minute, would you put yourself in a prison with spikes on the walls and on the floor in the hopes that your offender feels the pain? Absolutely not! When you do not forgive, you inevitably put yourself in that prison. Unforgiveness brings about bitterness, which induces depression, and it can even impact your health. A research was carried out in Concordia University to determine the relationship between failure, bitterness, and quality of life and it was determined that "*Persistent*

> *bitterness may result in global feelings of anger and hostility that, when strong enough, could affect a person's physical health,"* - Dr. Carsten Wrosch.

There is a famous saying that unforgiveness is like you drinking a bottle of poison in the hopes that your offender dies from it. To forgive is NOT the easiest thing to do but, it can be done; it is an act of the will, and only the strong can do it. You can do it, the fact that you are reading this page right now tells me that you are fighting for your precious life, that you have not given up hope. You are more than a CONQUEROR.

Find ways to cope with the hurt and pain. A friend of mine was deeply hurt and abused by her husband, but she found numerous ways to deal with it: on a personal level, with supernatural help from God, group meetings with fellow victims and eventually as she healed, she started her own nonprofit to prevent such abuse from happening to others. She found her purpose from her share of bad experiences. Bad things happen, but you chose your reaction! What will it be?

When life knocks you down, you ALWAYS have the right to choose from these three choices

To stay down, to fall further, or to get back up.

2

The lie you believe

"Nobody loves me."

This is the worse lie you can ever tell yourself! How can you possibly know that nobody loves you? Have you met everybody on the planet and not one person liked you? Sometimes we tend to make judgments on a whole based on our experience with too little that cannot even represent the smallest part of the whole. We all have experienced dislike and hatred by those who are supposed to love us, but that doesn't mean that they represent every other person we may come across. I will like for you to consider this scenario for a moment: how many car crashes do you witness daily? Does that imply that no one should ever drive a car because cars crash every day? Absolutely not! The car could be in perfect condition, but the condition of the driver could be impaired and vis versa. People can only give you what they have. Don't judge the whole, based on the few that mistreated you, look past their behaviors, and consider the fact that they are only giving what they have.

Now, what can someone do to prove to you that they love you? What will you consider the one thing that will give you the confident assurance that you are loved?

"Greater love has no one than he that lays down his life for a friend" – Jesus

"For God so love the world that he gave His only begotten Son" – John, a disciple of Jesus Christ.

God loves you so much, even though you may not know it. He loved you before you were born. He wanted to have a permanent relationship with you so much that He gave up His life to show you how much you mean to Him. You were worth His blood, and He painfully but lovingly and freely gave it all up for you! What a love, what a reckless love! You also must think about this beyond your own self. There is someone out there whom you haven't met yet who is waiting to love you and to be loved by you. If you give up now, then that person misses out on the love they would have received from you, and you, in turn, would never know what the love you are looking for would have felt like. Don't make a permanent decision because of a temporary situation.

If you give yourself a well-deserved chance, you'll find the love that will make what you think you're missing right now seem like nothing! You may say "well, the love I'm looking for is parental/family love. If my own can't love me, who will?"

Family is important in shaping and presenting to us the perspective from which we view ourselves, but there comes a time when you must determine and own how you see yourself. By the end of the day, you are responsible for loving yourself first, and you should do so, regardless of how others feel about you.

Lack of family love should not be the end of your life. It is hard to deal with, but it can be dealt with. King David, a famous character in the Bible, experienced family rejection. Due to the circumstances that surrounded his birth, he was considered a bastard and a nobody. He suffered innocently over the plight imposed on him by forces beyond his control.

David was not permitted to eat with the rest of his family but was assigned to a separate table in the corner. He was given the task of shepherding in the wildest part of the desert because they hoped that a wild beast would come and kill him while he was performing his duties thus, removing the shame of a bastard child from them. He experienced humiliation, bullying, and deep hurt, especially because it came from those who were supposed to love him- His family. David was a poor, heartbroken, and a love-starved boy, with no friend or shoulder to cry on. But, during all these depressing life situations he found solace in God; he rose up to become one of the most famous kings in Israel! Not only that, he managed to have so much love for himself and for people as well especially his family!

The truth you must accept

"I am loved by God!"

You may have been mistreated in many forms by those who are supposed to love and protect you, as a result of their irresponsibility or something that you may have done against them knowingly or unknowingly, and it deeply hurts. But know this: you can be healed from the hurt, but ask yourself, "How was our relationship in the past? When did things begin to go sour? Did I try to address issues when I started seeing signs of things going bad?" If you can, have a meeting with those involved and get to the root of the problem for the sake of peace. Do your due diligence to satisfy your conscience and hope that they can be a resolution, but, at the end of the day, you cannot control how people view and treat you. You are 100% responsible for your reactions; nobody has the right to make you feel unloved without your permission. Don't give anyone the pleasure of feeling that without their love, you cannot survive. Whether anyone loves or reject you, cannot and, should not have any impact on your worth and will to live. The love that matters is the love of God, your creator, the one whose love for you is everlasting. *"for I have loved you with an everlasting love"*- God

God loves you so much that he gave up his life for you, he didn't just profess his love, he carried out his love. If this doesn't make you feel ABSOLUTELY LOVED...

When you get just how much God loves you, you, in turn, will begin to love yourself and will have no desire to end the life you love!

There is this song that hits the nail on the head, it is titled "Reckless Love" by Cory Asbury. Watch his live performance of this song on YouTube, it will change your life.

Some friends stick closer than a brother- King Solomon

Remember that sometimes, family is not always bone and blood. King David in the story above despite being despised by his family had a friend called Jonathan, who saw so much value in him to the point that Jonathan was willing to go against his own father and his supposed heirship to his father's throne as king of Israel to protect his friendship with David. If you are patient, you will discover those who value and appreciate you being in their lives.

You are loved, those who are supposed to love you may not see it now but, always remember you are loved!

12/7/23

3

The lie you believe

"I have no value."

There is nothing more valuable than a human life! The question is, how do you define value? In the world today, most define value as the amount of money in your bank account, the designers you wear, the number of followers you have on social media, the list goes on. "Things" are hyped and promoted, and people begin to feel that if they do not have these "things," that there is little or no value to their lives. We have placed the cart before the horse, you need to understand that we are the ones that add value to anything and all things. Without people getting on social media, it becomes worthless; without people buying expensive cars, the cars rust away; without people to live in the big house, it deteriorates!

We are the value! Take people away, and the things that seem attractive becomes nothing. Now the value of a thing to you determines what you pay for it. If you feel something is worth $1 and it is priced for $5, you will not buy it; on the other hand, if you feel something is worth $5 and it is priced for $1, you will buy it and ask them to keep the change. The way you handle something is determined by the value you place on it, right? When you feel suicidal, it means that you have succeeded in convincing yourself that you have no value. But keep reading. I am about to prove to you just how valuable you are to God and to the world.

Forget what people say about you or what life has thrown at you. If a $100 bill came to you and said, "I have been squeezed and stamped on; therefore, I have lost my value." What will you say to that $100 bill? You'll say to it, "Don't say that, you are still a $100 bill, and you have value." The situations you go through in life CANNOT change your value. I know you have people you look up to, that may have said and done things that made you feel that you are not valuable or important but, who would you rather believe? Them, or the one who created you? Let me make it easy for you to get.

If all your friends and family said that you were a terrible singer and mock at you whenever you sang, but, you are convinced about your talents then, you decide to go for the X factor, you sing and get a standing ovation from the judges and the crowd, will it matter to you what your friends and family said? Absolutely not! The experts say you are a great singer, who cares what the rest think? If the experts had said that you couldn't sing, then you would have believed that of a truth you cannot sing. That's the way it is; what people say and do to you does not determine your worth and value. If God, your creator, your father says, that you were worthy of His death on the cross, that you are valuable and precious to Him then, who cares about the other voices who tell you otherwise. But the question in your heart is, "Why does God care so much for me?" A king in the ancient times named David, in one of his many songs, asked the same question because he couldn't understand what value he had. I mean, why would a great big God care about him when there are billions of people in the world! *"What is man that you are mindful of him?"* King David asked in one of his many songs.

Please allow me to explain to you why and how you are extremely valuable.

12/8/23

The truth you must accept

"I am extremely valuable."

Yes! You are. You are full of worth.

TRACING YOUR VALUE TO THE VERY BEGINNING

Then God said, "Let us make mankind in our image, in our likeness, so that they may rule over the fish in the sea and the birds in the sky, over the livestock and all the wild animals, and overall the creatures that move along the ground."

So, God created mankind in his own image, in the image of God he created them;   male and female he created them.
– Moses, a prophet of God

The way we were thought in Sunday school for those who went to church was, "On the sixth day, God created man," and that's it. We just know that God created us; we have no idea how and why He made us in the way He did. So, all these years, we walk around with the barest minimum idea about who and how we are.

Let's look deeply into our uniqueness and value. God created us in His image and likeness. The image of God doesn't necessarily only mean his physic and stature but, His seal upon us. Just like you would have the seal or logo on any product put there by the manufacturer. Look at an iPhone; without being told, by reason of that seal on the product, you can come to a reasonable conclusion that the product was made by Apple.

The likeness of God, on the other hand, symbolizes His essence, His character, and DNA. For example, God is a creator, so just like our father, we also create amazing things, like cars, planes, and magnificent buildings. God is a giver. So, like our father, we derive joy in giving. He is just, so we have a sense of justice within us, in other words, we have the nature of God residing in us and, whether we know Him or not, that nature is in there, always. Just like the blood type or DNA of a rebellious child doesn't change because he rebelled against his parents, it is with us. We have some inbuilt nature of God in us. God values us because we carry His nature. Another good example is dominion; God has dominion and, He gave us dominion over all that he had made. The question is **if He didn't see value in us, why would He entrust such a huge responsibility on us?** Think about this for a moment.

Also, we are both created and made. The word "create" comes from the Hebrew word Barra meaning, to make something out of nothing, and the word "make" also stems from the Hebrew word Asa meaning, something made from existing material. God first created the spirit, and then, for us to be able to occupy the earth, he made from the dust of the ground, a body, and put the spirit into the clay he molded from the ground (our bodies). So, we humans, have two sources, the spirit in us comes from God, and the body comes from the ground. **Another reason why God values you so much is that you come from Him.**

We come directly from God, and this is how I know! When He wanted to create the fishes, He called them out of the sea, "**Then God said, "Let the waters swarm with fish and other life**"- Moses, a prophet of God.

When he wanted to create the plants, He called them out of the ground **"Then God said, "Let the land sprout with vegetation—every sort of seed-bearing plant, and trees that grow seed-bearing fruit**"- Moses, a prophet of God.

When He wanted to make us, He called us straight out of Himself. He said **"Let us make man in our image and likeness**"- and **He brought us out of Himself, that's why He loves us so much, that's why we are so valuable to Him.** Just like a mother loves the baby that she just bore! Do you understand now that you are valuable?

For some of you who are atheists, who believe that you just suddenly appeared here from nothing and are just occupying space and that there is no purpose for your life, please think about these questions.

- Do you truly believe the scientific impossibilities that nothing created everything?

- Can you in the history of this earth point out a time that an explosion created such perfect order?

- Do you believe that an author wrote this book, that a builder built where you live in or that a painter painted that beautiful artwork you love so much?

- Isn't it only rational to conclude that creation has a creator? - God

The moment you realize that you are not a product of a big bang, simply existing with no purpose or hope then, you will have a paradigm shift because you will now understand that your life has a purpose and high value.

"Before I formed you in the womb, I knew you, I set you apart"- God

"Even the hairs on your head are numbered, fear not, you are of more value than many sparrows"- Jesus

12/11/23

4

The lie you believe

"This is the only way out of my problems."

"There is a way that seems right to a man but, the end leads to destruction"- King Solomon

To be honest with you, suicide is not the way out of your problems but the start of an unending one. You need to realize that your life is not your own; it was given to you by God, so, in other words, you will be committing the murder of self. Do you really want to meet God on those terms? Think about this.

There is always a solution to any kind of problem in the world. Just because you have not yet found the solution doesn't mean that it doesn't exist. You owe it to yourself to find the solution. There is nothing new under the sun. Whatever you are going through right now, someone else has gone through it and has overcome it!

"What has been will be again, what has been done will be done again; there is nothing new under the sun" – King Solomon

31

"No temptation has overtaken you, except what is common to mankind. And God is faithful; He will not let you be tempted beyond what you can bear. But, when you are tempted, he will also provide a way out so that you can endure it." – Paul, an apostle of Jesus Christ

There is a way out of your problems, but suicide is not that way. Stop looking within you because clearly, you do not have the answer, and that's why you are about to throw in the towel and give up your life that would eventually turn out to be very wonderful. God is the way out, you have tried everything else, how about giving God a try.

"I am the way, the truth, and the life…"- Jesus Christ

12/12/23

The truth you must accept

"There is a way, I just haven't found it yet."

Be patient with yourself; life is not a race. It's a process; if you can't find a way today, you will find it tomorrow. If you seek with the intention of finding, as opposed to the intention of proving that there is no way out, you will find a way. Someone out there has the solution to your problem; there is an organization that was created with your situation in mind and even if there is none, well, here is an opportunity for you to be hope for someone else.

Thomas Edison tried 1,000 times before he was able to get the light bulb that we all enjoy today in different shapes and forms. I'm sure at some point, he and others around him must have said, "There is no way this is ever going to work" but, that did not make him give up, and, today, we are enjoying the fruit of his perseverance. Have you tried to find a way 100 times? Nothing worthy of value and celebration is ever gotten overnight, think of the depths that must be drilled before oil is gotten from the ground. What you have inside of you is worth trying 10,000 times over!

Sometimes you feel that ending your life is the only way out because you haven't found that thing that is worth living for, but if you wait a little longer and try a little harder, you will find what you have been looking for and surprisingly, you'll find that it has been much closer to you than you imagined. There is hope, there is light, you may not see it or feel it now, but it is closer than you think.

God will make a way, where there seems to be no way. He walks in ways you cannot see. He will make way for you. He will be your guide, hold you closely to his side, with love and strength for each new day He will make a way, He will make a way – Don Moen, American musician

"God is our refuge and strength, a very present help in times of need"- King David

"For everyone who calls on the name of the Lord will be saved"- Paul, an apostle of Jesus Christ

Will you do that today?

5

The lie you believe

"There is no purpose for my life."

The lack of knowledge of the presence of a thing doesn't imply the absence of it. There is a reason for your existence. No one is purposeless; you are the answer to someone's problems, you are hope to someone's hopelessness. When God created you, He did so intentionally, but you are responsible for discovering what that reason is, and I can help you know exactly what you were created for.

"Before I formed you in your mother's womb, I knew you, I ordained you a prophet to the nations" – God

Truth is, if you think a bit deeper, the reason you want to commit suicide may be where your purpose lies. You can find purpose in your pain so, instead of wallowing in your situation and convincing yourself that you are the only one going through it, ask yourself, "How many people are going through this? Are they thinking what I'm thinking? How can I help?"

Alright, now get a pen and a paper and write down the answers to these questions sincerely.

1. What qualities do people appreciate the most about you?

2. What are you passionate about?

3. How do you want to be remembered?

4. When you look at the world today, what are the top three problems you see that makes you cringe, that makes you say, "Someone must do something about this." Your current suffering may be as a result of one or more of the problems because it remains unsolved in the world. Because you are a victim of unsolved problems in the world doesn't mean you end your life for it; it should rather start a fire in your soul to begin to find solutions to them. It may not be a solution that goes viral, but it will solve the problems one day at a time for someone who is a victim of that problem. Remember, little grains of sand, little drops of water make a mighty ocean. You may have been created and set apart for such a problem as this. Look at the big picture. What problems can you solve?

5. If you had no personal struggles and had all the money in the world, which of the top 3 problems will give you so much fulfillment when you solve it?

6. Write 10 things you can do today to help solve the number one problem on your list

Do you see that there is a solution that you were created to solve? Instead of letting problems end you why not arise like the hero you are and begin to positively impact the world in the small ways that you can. The world needs what you carry and will completely miss out if you do not deliver up all the fantastic solutions in you for it.

12/18/23

The truth you must accept

"There is a purpose for my life, I just haven't discovered it yet."

What must you do now to discover your purpose? You have stared already by writing down the answers to the above questions now; you must spend some time and think deeply about these problems and begin to write down up to ten steps you can take today to start solving those problems, number one being, staying alive!

HOW TO START FULFILLING YOUR PURPOSE?

See yourself as one who has water to give to a group of dehydrated people whose lives are totally dependent on you. If you die, they die.

This is what it'll take to deliver up that water.

1. **THINK ABOUT YOUR PASSION –** The ability to think is a potent tool possessed by any human doing it right. It put things into perspective for you, it shapes your life. As you think, so you become. So, Let your thinking be productive, the kind that will clear your doubt and will help you see better. Let your thinking be the kind that will allow you to come clean with yourself. Let your thinking be focused and not scattered. Decide what you want to think about and

focus your thoughts on every aspect of your subject. Let your thinking be positive and not negative, ask yourself, will my passion help others, will it make me a better person, will it give me a reason to live daily no matter how hard life gets?

2. **BELIEVE IN YOUR PASSION-** If you do not believe strongly in your passion, you will not succeed in it, you must understand that you are unique. Don't desire to do what someone else is doing, instead believe that you can make a difference with what you have on the inside. Be your own cheerleader! Your faith in your passion triggers the fire in you to move to the next step, which is, ACTION!

3. **DO-** No matter how much you think and believe, it all avails to nothing if you don't act on it. You may feel heavy on the inside, and you may even convince yourself that you cannot afford to move but, the moment you take that first step, you'll realize that you can.

4. **GO SLOW-** One of the significant discouragement people face is the fact that they are not where the unrealistically expect to be. We live in a microwave society right now, where we want to happen in our lives today what is meant to happen in the next five years and, when the process doesn't move as quick as they expect, there comes discouragement, complaining, and depression. Don't let anyone on

social media and those overnight success stories drive you to think that your life is not good or that you are living behind the schedule of life. Nothing of great worth that leaves lasting impact on the sands of time happens overnight; if your purpose and your dreams are worth it then do not rush it. Take your time, do your due diligence and keep at it every day. Money and fame can happen overnight, but wealth and legacy takes a lifetime.

5. **FOCUS –** What you focus on will thrive; you can have a dream, believe in it, and start it, but if your focus is not committed to that dream of yours, it will slowly die on you. Don't do too many things at the same time. Pick the one thing you are truly passionate about. If you spread yourself too thin, you will get easily exhausted even from the things you love, and that will cause you to begin to question your passion. You may be multi-talented and a great multi-tasker and may feel like you are under-delivering on your passions by doing only one thing, but don't be bothered by that. Your passion is yours and if it is truly yours it will stick with you like white on rice. A time is coming when you will be able to easily do more than one thing at a time without breaking your back, but for now pick one, how do you know the one? If you were given $10 million and were told that you could only do one of your many

passions for the next 10 years of your life, which one will you pick?

You are important, you are needed, please stay alive for us and fulfill your purpose!

12/19/23

6

The lie you believe

"I have done too many bad things."

Let me tell you this, you are absolutely loved by God! His love for you is reckless and extravagant. There is no bad you have done that is beyond His forgiveness while you are alive. Name any kind of sin in the world ever committed by man! No sin is greater than His love, this promise can only be assessed by the living, not the dead, but if you die with the guilt of all the wrong things you have done, you will be judged based on them. But while you are on earth, He is willing and able to forgive you no matter, and I say again, no matter the weight of your sins.

"For, if you confess your sins to God, He is faithful and just to forgive you"- John, a disciple of Jesus Christ

You may scoff at this as you say, "You don't know what I have done" but, there is hope for you, you don't have to be weighed down by the guilt of the things you have done. The only thing that will hinder you from going to God is shame. Remember when you were much younger, when you did something wrong, how you would run and hide from your parents or guardians? Shame is the feeling of unworthiness and self-rejection; it is normal when we have acted out of our God-like nature, and our conscience convicts us of our wrongdoing, and we simply want to punish ourselves for our wrong doings. But you don't have to punish yourself. You can deal with your guilt healthily and move past it.

1/2/24

The truth you must accept

"There is forgiveness for me."

Before you deal with guilt, you must first understand the purpose of guilt. It's like your smoke detector. When smoke is detected the alarm rings and you are alerted of a threat to your property and life which helps you address the issue swiftly, imagine if your smoke detector was not functioning, and you were fast asleep, and your house was on fire. You could lose your precious life because your alarm didn't ring right? This is the purpose of your conscience and guilt, it alerts your heart when you have done wrong. But it will be an error if after the situation has been assessed and dealt with, the alarm keeps ringing, then we must find a way to fix that stupid alarm that keeps ringing when there is no cause for it to ring. The alarm has done its duty by alerting you via the guilt you feel, now how do we stop that alarm from ringing and giving you a headache? First, you must know the cause of the guilt and be honest with yourself about it. What is the magnitude of the wrong you did and how did it affect you and those impacted by it? Are you hiding from the law because of it, have you been ostracized from your family because of it? No matter the situation you find yourself in, if you can apologize please do so immediately. Call, text, send a note; whichever means of communication you choose, be absolutely sincere in your apology. It will be up to the offended to accept your apology or not. The next thing you must do is ask God for forgiveness. You can be forgiven of all your shortcomings because you have a good father who loves you beyond your sins. His grace is greater than all your sins.

"Come now let us reason together says the Lord, though your sins are like crimson I will make it white as wool, though it like scarlet I will make it white as snow" – God

I, even I, am He who blots out your transgression for my own sake; and I will not remember your sins- God

God is not just the Big Guy up in the sky with a hammer ready to hit us at the sight of sin. He is your loving father. He will accept you with all your badness, forgive you if you ask Him and then, draw you closer to His side. His answer when you ask for His forgiveness is ALWAYS, yes! He will forgive and remove the guilt and shame, and you will become a brand-new person. You may be experiencing the physical consequences for your wrongdoings like jail time and other side effects, but to God you are as free as the wind and as pure as a newborn. Do you now see the hope you have? Now, close your eyes and sincerely confess your sins to God, your Daddy, and ask Him to forgive you as you repent of them.

"The sacrifice God wants is a willing spirit. God will not reject a heart that is broken and sorry for its sin" – King David

"Let the wicked forsake his ways, and the unrighteous man his thoughts; let him return to God, for he will abundantly pardon"- Isaiah, a prophet of God

Now, forgive yourself, the earlier you do this, the better for you. I understand you feel a sense of justice when you hold on to your guilt, but that guilt is long overdue; it is an overstayed guest, and it will suck the life out of you, and keep you depressed! The moment you felt remorse and apologized, its job was done! So, you must get rid of it by forgiving yourself. If God can lovingly forgive you, why do you think you cannot forgive yourself? This is just a trick of the devil whose job in your life is to steal, kill, and destroy; don't let him win. Everyone makes terrible mistakes that if they had the power, they would turn back the hands of time, stop beating yourself up. You are already forgiven! Accept it now.

1/3/24

7
The lie you believe

"I am too weak to handle life's challenges."

You are anything but weak, and I can prove it. A few months before you were born you were in a race. There were about 500 million sperm racing for the egg in your mother's womb. Of all the other millions of sperm, you had the strength to beat the others and then fertilize the egg (Did you smile a bit?)

Life has a way of dealing with us all and I believe the hard things come to the toughest not the weakest of people. The situation with the world today is that we think we can do life on our own. We assume that we are self-sufficient, but we are not. We are frail with limited strengths. We cannot do life on our own; there is a higher power who is willing to help us carry on from where our strength fails. *"For a person does not prevail by his own strength"* – Samuel, a prophet of God

"Come to me, all of you who are weary and carry heavy burdens, and I will give you rest" –Jesus

God wants to help you through your weak moments. We were meant to live life in partnership with God, our creator, who knows how to repair and restore us when we are broken and recharge our strength when we are weak. You have tried your own abilities, your friends and families, therapies, and psychiatrist, different religions but, all to no avail, how about you call on Jesus?

"Everyone who calls, 'Help, God!' gets help."- Paul, an apostle of Jesus Christ

"Cast all your anxieties on Him because He cares for you" – Peter, an apostle of Jesus Christ

Life will give you a fight, punch you in the gut and, before you hit the ground it kicks you in the head, and while you are trying to recover it gives you another blow on the skull that can render you unconscious. Yes, life will sometimes knock you down, but you and only you can decide to surrender to your feelings of weakness and then give up or, show life what you are made of. The truth is, no matter how beat up the hero of a movie is, we know that somehow, he will overcome the villain one way or another. In this life, you are the hero. How do you want your movie to end? Do You want to exit as a coward, or do you want to "HAPPEN" to life? I hope you choose the latter.

The truth you must accept

"I am stronger than the urge to take my precious life."

"Let the weak say I am strong" -Joel, a prophet of God

"Do not fear, do not be dismayed, for I am your God, I will strengthen you"- God

"He gives strength to the weary and increases the power of the weak"- Isaiah a prophet of God

Saying you are strong when you are weak is not a lie, but the truth that your subconscious wants your conscious state to accept because it is true. Because you feel weak doesn't mean you should accept it as your fact! Feelings come, and feelings go; don't make an irreversible decision because of a reversible feeling. You are strong. You are a warrior, and you have the armies of heaven willing to back you up, if you ask. You can win this fight.

The reason people chant mantras is that they want to get the truth of who they are and what they really believe to align with their current state of mind. Your unconscious reality is that you are strong, your current state is that you are weak, so, I want you to say to yourself "I am strong, I am a warrior, this depression will not see the end of me, I will tell my story to help others." Repeat this to yourself every day!

1/8/24

8

The lie you believe

"I will gain peace this way."

You will not gain peace this way; you will only be running away from the problems that you could have conquered if you fought. The challenge most of us have is that we do not want to accept the fact that we did not make ourselves, and therefore we cannot fix ourselves when we are broken into pieces. There is a peace that comes from only God, your father.

In this life, there will always be chaos, troubles, and disasters, but does that mean that we run from it when it happens around us? No! God promised that He can give us the peace that passes all understanding, not as the world gives. Meaning that, the peace of the world is conditional; as long as you have money in your account, your family is in good shape, you're not in the hospital, you have friends that love you as so on. But, when one or more of these things on which you base your peace on goes away, so goes your peace also.

The peace that God can give you is the peace that keeps you calm even in the storms of life; everything can fall apart in your life, but in your heart is such a peace that those around you cannot understand. The same thing happened with Jesus when He was in a boat with his disciples, and the storm began to rage, everyone was panicked in the boat, and they began to look for Jesus. When they found him, He was fast asleep; they woke Him up and questioned Him saying "Do you not care that we are going to die?" They could not understand how He was not impacted by the storm even though He was amid the storm. This kind of peace is what God wants to give you; you cannot find it on your own. You can have peace right here and now no matter what you are going through. I want you to do something for me now.

Close this book for a moment, forget your pride for a moment, forget all the chaos as well. You've tried medication, therapies, and all, right? Okay, go on your knees, and sincerely ask Jesus to give you peace, the kind of peace He exhibited when he was on that boat that was about to get wrecked. You can read the whole story, it's in the Bible, the book of Mark chapter 4 verses 35 to 41. It will help you in your current situation. Trust Him with your heart. If you fight long enough, you will see the end of the chaos in your life as opposed to the chaos seeing your end. I challenge you to fight, hold on and try Jesus!

01/09/24

The truth you must accept

"I can have peace here and now."

You can, if you want to, and I know that somewhere deep down in your heart, you really want to find peace. So, will you let life happen to you, or will you show life what you are made of? I know you will choose the latter.

Cast all your anxiety on Him for he cares for you- Peter, a disciple of Jesus Christ

"And the peace of God which transcends all understanding will guard your heart and minds in Christ Jesus. – Paul, a disciple of Jesus Christ

"He gives strength to his people; He blesses his people with peace" – King David

It's not about the raging storms in your life, but it's about who you have with you in the storm. Jesus is the prince of peace, and he can flood your life with peace right now!

1/10/24

9

The lie you believe

"I can't help it, it's a medical condition."

According to the John Hopkins study, it is estimated that over 250,000 Americans die each year from medical mistakes, that would rank behind heart disease and cancer which in 2014 took each, 600,000 lives. Considering this humongous medical error, I believe that we are safe to say that doctors can make mistakes in their diagnosis.

Johns Hopkins researchers found that "diagnostic errors — not surgical mistakes or medication overdoses — accounted for the largest fraction of claims, the most severe patient harm, and the highest total of penalty payouts. Diagnosis-related payments amounted to $38.8 billion between 1986 and 2010."

Researchers estimate the number of patients suffering misdiagnosis-related, potentially preventable, significant permanent injury, or death annually in the United States ranges from 80,000 to 160,000.

You are not mental

I want to assure you that you are not mental; you are human. Life in itself is depressing. Think about it: Every time you turn on the news, there is a report of shooting, natural disaster, babies dying in cars, shootings that makes you consider buying bulletproof vests for your entire family to wear the next time you want to go the movies or Wal-Mart. You lose your job, your business collapses, the people you love the most get so sick to the point of inactivity, or even worse, they die! Any way you think of it, life is so depressing. It only becomes dangerous when you allow the negativities around you to have a strong hold on you.

Think about this for a while: what happened in your life that pushed you into depression? Was it war, rape, sex change, domestic violence, bullying, drugs, broken relationships, constant failure, betrayal, occultic activities, crimes, insecurities about your physical appearance, social media pressure, loss of a loved one, struggles of single parenting, loss of a body part, having a baby or guilt? Think about it some more: what kind of books were you reading, what kind of movies were you watching, what kind of music were you listening to? Think about all these for a while. You had an experience that instigated all the emotions of shame, guilt, unworthiness, low self-esteem, feelings of a failure, anger, disappointment, loneliness, bitterness to name a few, that brings about depression as they linger in your heart.

In as much as science has tried to medicate depression, we are experiencing a high rise in depression in our society today; doesn't this tell you something? The absolute cure for depression is not in any pills on the planet, besides, most of them come with side effects that we are all trying to avoid suicidal thoughts!

Time magazine published,

"Treating depression is a major challenge, since among the millions of people affected worldwide only 1 in 5 tend to respond well to anti-depressant and for many people who are eventually helped by drugs it can take months even years of cycling through the various medication to find the one that works best. In the meantime, their depression persists and sometimes worsens."

80 out of every 100 who are suffering from clinical depression don't find help with drugs. Many even get worse owing to side effects.

In this life, we cannot escape troubles; it is part of life on this planet as we know it. Some have more than others. Some find the strength to overcome their problems and some don't.

Do you believe in miracles? You may, you may not, but if you have tried everything on the doctors' list and have seen no result, what do you have to lose if you try the one who created you and therefore knows how to fix your brokenness?

1/11/24

The truth you must accept

"There is healing for me."

No matter the state you're in, God can heal and deliver you. He already made provision for your healing; all you need to do in response is, ask for healing and believe.

"Seek and you will find, ask and you will receive, knock and the door will be opened for you" – Jesus

You may say I don't have time for faith, "Am I just going to get well simply because I ask and believe?" My answer to that is, yes! That is all you need to do. You already exercise faith every day; when you take the pills doctors prescribe or when you trust your life to a pilot. You already have faith, all you need to do is place it on God, it is not easy because we live in a "see to believe world" but God wants you to believe to see. Let me define faith:

"Faith shows the reality of what we hope for; it is the evidence of things we cannot see" – Paul, an apostle of Jesus

All you need to do is ask and believe for your healing, it is so close to you but only your faith can activate the healing power to begin to work in your life. It is that simple!

"Everything is possible for the one who believes" - Jesus

"But He was pierced for our transgressions, He was crushed for our iniquities; the punishment that brought us peace was

on Him, and by His wounds we are healed"- Isaiah, a prophet of God

The above scripture was prophesying what Jesus was going to go through on the cross, it was written 750 years before Jesus came to the scene, it is such a powerful verse because it says you ARE healed already. Receive it, believe it, activate it in your life. Now, I am not insinuating that you disregard your doctors but, as you work with your doctors continue to believe God for healing as well and, He will make all things work together for your good.

Over the years, as I have grown in my relationship with Jesus, I have seen and heard of many miraculous healings, from a drug addict quitting overnight without any therapy, to a woman with HIV cured in one day! You too can be healed!

When it comes to getting anything from God, many times you will have to take off your scientific and rational hat off and just trust him like a kid. This kind of faith is called a child-like faith.

Jesus died on the cross not just so we can be forgiven of our sins, but that we can also be healed from our diseases. He cares about all facets of our health; He gave us full coverage!

"I will restore you to health and heal your wounds, says the Lord" – God

Listen to this song by Don Moen "I am the Lord your healer" on you tube and play on repeat! Sing along and see what happens. I challenge you!

61/12/24

How to destroy suicidal thoughts

"You cannot stop a bird from flying over your head but, you can stop it from building a nest on your head"- African proverbs

We all have thoughts and hear negative voices that tell us to do things we know we shouldn't do. Truth is we are not left without the power to choose. You either silence that voice, or you give it the power to be amplified in your heart by paying attention to it. You either starve that voice, or you meditate on it but, the more you meditate on it, the more it digs deep into your heart and takes you captive, mercilessly. The time in thoughts you give to the negative voice, the more it grows and soon engulfs you to the point that you struggle to breathe.

If you ever watched Tom and Jerry cartoon, then, you must remember a time when either Tom or Jerry is in a sticky situation and then two little creature appears on each shoulder, one, a positive voice that is clothed in white with wings and a halo, the other, a negative voice clothed in red with pointy tails, a horn, and a three-prong fork, both contending for the heart of the subject, but all they can do is be convincing in their argument of what it is they want you to do. The choice is up to the subject. The angel or demon cannot force you against your will; you only go with whoever convinces and makes the most sense to you.

Truth is, we all have voices in our head demanding our submission. I have been on the highway several times driving at 75 miles per hour, and I hear a voice suggesting that I just make a quick swerve and see what it will feel like but, I shut that stupid voice up and then it shuts up. Even Jesus got tempted to throw himself off a mountain, but He rebuked the negative voice. Because you hear voices doesn't imply that you do what it asks you to do, especially when you know that it will end badly.

Most people feel powerless about the voices because they don't know that they have the power to override it. The truth is, the "voices" are no respecter of anyone, it will try its luck on anyone in the hopes that someone will fall victim, but you have the power to shut down those voices. There are things that you do that empowers or subdues the voices in your head; the things you watch, read and listen to go a long way when it comes to strengthening or weakening that negative voice in your head.

DROWN THE VOICE WITH ANOTHER VOICE

BUT HOW?

1. **Cast it down:** "Casting down imaginations, and every high thing that exalts itself against the knowledge of God, and bringing into captivity every

> thought to the obedience of Christ" – Paul, a disciple
> of Jesus Christ

Every human is hunted by evil imaginations all the time! That is why God instructs us to cast it down. When that voice comes and tells you lies about who you are and your situation, you need to stand your ground and cast in down. When it speaks negatively, you, in turn, speak positively.

For every lie that voice tells you, you must counter it with the truth. But what is the truth? The truth about you is in the manual for your life: The Bible, well, unless you believe the scientific impossibility that nothing made everything. Just like you would use the manual of your fridge or dishwasher when you cannot figure out how to fix it, so you can check out the manual that contains the way to fix your life, and the manual for your life is the Bible.

Just like every creator puts a manual in his product so that the consumers know how to take care and troubleshoot their product, so did God. The truth about your worth, value and how to handle every situation in your life is in His words, and that is what that crazy negative voice in your head is afraid of. This is your weapon to defeat that voice, and it is at your disposal; grab hold of it, and don't let that voice laugh over your defeat!

"For as a man thinks, so he becomes"- King Solomon

The more you dwell on those negative thoughts, the more your life aligns with it. Life is like this: your output cannot be different from your input, and what you feed and pay attention to will grow! As you think on what the negative voices say, you begin to believe it, and your wrong beliefs activate the power of the negative forces that makes your life become exactly what you think.

"Finally, brothers and sisters, whatever is true, whatever is noble, whatever is right, whatever is pure, whatever is lovely, whatever is admirable—if anything is excellent or praiseworthy—think about such things"- Paul, an apostle of Jesus Christ

1. **Listen to worship songs:** It has been scientifically proven that music has a way of impacting your mood, stress level, and even your subconscious mind. One of the best ways to influence culture is through music. It is a universal soul language; you agree with the message it presents, unknowingly, as you nod your head to the beat, its message sinks deep into a part of you where mere talk cannot reach. Every musician is inspired by something negative or positive, and you invoke the spirit or emotions that inspired the singer when you sing or play their song, and it begins to impact you. Music is more spiritual than physical, that is why it can influence how you feel, think, and act.

When you listen to Christian worship songs, it gives you hope, it reminds you of your value, it draws you closer to God and makes you think about His love. The kind of music you listen to in these dark times of your life can either take you deeper into the darkness or bring light and hope to you.

The link to bad music and suicide has happened too many times to be considered a coincidence. Here are some stories of people who have been influenced to commit suicide by the kind of music they listen to.

In 1975, 16-year-old John Tanner, listening to acid rock and smoking marijuana, drew deeper and deeper into a depressed state. On January 13, he loaded his 12-gauge shotgun with a slug and set it against the chimney in his room, his mind filled with thoughts of suicide.

On January 15, he skipped school and listened to rock music all day, especially Black Sabbath's *Paranoid* album. At 5:15 p.m. he put his shotgun to his chin and pulled the trigger. Though much of his face was blasted away, he lived through the horrible ordeal, and his face was painfully reconstructed in 20 surgeries over 10 years at the cost of $300,000. By his own testimony, his involvement in heavy metal music quickly led to drug abuse, rebellion against his elders, depression, and thoughts of self-destruction. He could quote the nihilistic lyrics to Black Sabbath's "Killing Yourself to Live" by heart. "The execution of your mind, you really have to learn/ You're wishing that the hands of doom could take your mind away/ And you don't care if you don't see again the light of day." Happily, after Tanner shot himself, he received Jesus Christ as his Savior (*Why Knock Rock?* pp. 161, 162).

One of the Scorpions' songs advocated suicide, describing it as flying "over the rainbow." When a 17-year-old in North Carolina killed himself by jumping from a bridge onto Interstate 40, thirty feet below, he left a suicide note saying, "I wouldn't mind if someone would write the Scorpions and tell them their No. 1 fan has left. Tell them I've flown to the rainbow" (*The Raleigh Times*, Raleigh, North Carolina, Feb. 13, 1986).

I know something deep down inside you wants to live so. I want you to discard that music that is making you sink deeper into this depressed state and start giving yourself life. Here is a list of my top 5 songs to shine light into your darkness right now. Listen to them:

- Reckless Love by Cory Asbury

- Good Father by Chris Tomlin

- Not Alone by Kari Jobe

- King of My Heart by Steffany Gretzinger

- No longer a slave to Fear by Chris Tomlin

Remember, you give out what you put in. These songs will illuminate your life.

2. **Pray:** This may be one of the hardest things to do when you are depressed, and I think it's because you

don't really understand the concept of prayers. Prayers simply mean humbling yourself, trusting in the love of God, and spilling your heart to Him.

Is anyone of you in trouble? He should pray- James, a disciple of Jesus

"Do not be anxious about anything, but in everything, by prayer and petition, with thanksgiving, present your request to God."- Paul and Timothy, disciples of Jesus Christ

*"We do not make requests of you because we are righteous, but because of your great mercy."-*Daniel, a prophet of God and special adviser to several Persian kings in Babylon

"This is the confidence we have in approaching God: that if we ask anything according to his will, he hears us." – John, a disciple of Jesus Christ

Call on God, and I GUARANTEE that He will answer you.

3. **Don't isolate yourself:** We were meant to live life in collaboration with God and with others. The more you separate yourself from the right people, the more you sink into loneliness, and the only company you will have is the negative voices in your head. The negative voices become louder and louder because there are no other voices competing with it. Talk to and with someone you trust, some people have gone through what you are going through right now—sometimes even worse—and they have come out of it. Search for such people and talk to them.

4. **Submit, then resist:** *"Submit yourself to God, resist the devil, and he will flee from you"* – James, a disciple of Jesus Christ

5. The only way to always overcome suicidal thoughts is to permanently submit yourself to God, your creator, and your father. The phrase "resist the devil" means to withstand, strive against, to cause him to "run away" from us. Resisting the devil must be accompanied by submitting to God. If you are not submitted to God, then you automatically are submitting to the devil; there is no in-between and, you cannot resist who you are submitted to because, by reason of your submission, they have authority over you. Submit yourself to God and begin to enjoy your victory.

DOES GOD CARE FOR THE DEPRESSED?

God understands that people get depressed but, beyond understanding the pain, He also offers hope and a way out.

GOD CARES

"The Lord is near to the brokenhearted and saves the crushed in spirit" – King David

God has a special place in His heart for the brokenhearted and crushed in spirit. When you find yourself under a crushing burden, God draws *near* to you. He sees you during your affliction and moves toward you with deliverance. Even though you can't feel His presence, God is nearer to you now than ever.

GOD IS YOUR HOPE

"Why is my soul cast down? Why so disturbed within me? Put your hope in God"- King David

I understand that you feel crushed, broken, downhearted, overwhelmed, and like there is no hope for tomorrow. But even though it *feels* like you have no hope for tomorrow, you DO have hope because God is your salvation. He will NEVER fail. I mean, you hoped in medication, in therapies, and in a human being who is apt to mistakes. Why will you not hope in the one who will never fail?

GOD IS YOUR LIFTER

"Humble yourself therefore under God's mighty hand that he may lift you up in due time, cast all your anxiety on him because he cares for you" - Peter, a disciple of Jesus Christ

When you are in a pit, in the bottom of the bottoms, you need someone above to give you a hand, to pull you up, just kick your pride to the curb and lift up your hands and I promise God will lift you up out of the pit of depression. He is reaching out right now, ready to pull you out but, He needs your permission. Will you let him?

1/15/24

CONSEQUENCE OF SUICIDE

"Or do you not know that your body is the temple of the Holy Spirit who is in you, whom you have from God, and you are not your own?"- Paul, a disciple of Jesus Christ

"Thou shalt not kill"- God

1. ETERNAL REGRETS

You did not create yourself; you have an owner, a creator. You did not give yourself life so, you have no right to take it. It will be murder, the murder of self, and I know that you wouldn't want to meet your creator on the terms of self-murder. You belong to Him and, He also can be yours if you ask Him. I know these words seem harsh but, it is coming from a place of deep love. I would rather slap you to heaven than kiss you to hell.

"Faithful are the wounds of a friend, but deceitful are the kisses of an enemy" - King Solomon

2. YOUR FAMILY GOES THROUGH THE SUFFERING AND PAIN OF LOOSING YOU

I heard the story of a woman who was suffering from a serious domestic violence situation and was depressed as a result of it, she went through numerous therapies but still wanted to take her life because she was just done! She was emotionally beaten and mentally drained. One day she left her baby in his crib, went out to her balcony in the apartment where she lived with her abusive husband at the time and was ready to jump, but the thought of her son and the fact that the man who was abusing her would have to be the one to raise him made her pause, she imagined what her child's future would look like without her and story that would be told of her and how her suicide would impact her son's view on life and the pains that comes with it, then she realized that her desire to live was greater than the pain she was going through. That was how she was able to overcome that suicidal thought on that fateful day.

There are thousands of families that are suffering from depression because their loved ones committed suicide, they wonder, "was I not worth her staying alive for?" "Did he not love me?" "Did I do something to cause this?" And its unfortunate that they will never know the answers to the many questions that hunts them when ever they think of their loved ones.

I know that in that moment when you feel like there is no point living on, that the last thing on your mind is "Family" and you are not able to be rational because the pain and hurt you go through beclouds your judgment and even pins your survival instincts down, but in as much as we can justify the legitimate pain of our hurt when very dark and negative things happen to us, we can also justify the will to fight through and what those who love us can do to see us come out victorious against suicidal thoughts.

01/16/24

SUICIDE SURVIVOR TESTAMENT

I JUST WANTED MY VERY IMPERFECT LIFE BACK!

"What made me do it? Honestly, I felt really lost. It felt like I was in a very dark haze, and even if I could see a way out, it was going to take a while to get out. I just didn't want to go through what I had gone through before; I didn't want to feel the pain. You see, I had just broken up with the only man I was seeing and was providing financial support for me. I was so scared; I didn't want to go back to being super broke or not having anyone to talk to or someone that checks on me. I felt alone, lost, broken and broke. The feeling of loneliness, it's the worst feeling, so I thought. I took a handful of some sleeping pills, and then I reduced it to half. I wonder what would have happened if I took it all? I should have called someone; I should have gone for a walk, or I should I watched a movie, pray, or just anything to get my mind off it.

When I woke up 2 hours after I took those pills, it was the worst feeling in the world. Then I realized that nothing was as crucial as life; all my worries and troubles where nothing but just specks compared to how precious life is. I had made a big moulid, regretted what I did with all my heart. I felt my spirit slipping out of me. I couldn't focus, and if my friend wasn't around, I could have died. I started asking God for forgiveness, and I felt my heart beating so fast. I couldn't concentrate on anything. Nothing is worth hurting yourself for. Once there is life there is hope. At the hospital, I felt so embarrassed because I know what had happened, but I couldn't bring myself to tell anyone. I just wanted my very imperfect life back. The one I had so much despised and wasn't grateful for. That feeling of being so cold and feeling like I couldn't breathe. The oxygen mask on my mouth made it clear that I had made a big mistake.

I got back home, and I felt fortunate that nothing terrible had happened.

Don't allow the devil to think you're not good enough or that nothing would get better. Life is priceless.

I kept on thanking God for saving me.

DONT THINK ABOUT HURTING YOURSELF. You think your life is bad until you realize that You can't put a price tag on Life. Talk to someone when you're feeling down.

Go on a walk, Pray"- Shalom B.

1/17/24

I KNOW YOUR STORY

Once, there was a rich man who lost a dollar and became frantic about it. He said to His employees, "I have lost a dollar, and I must find it." His employees all thought it was a prank, but the boss had never pulled anything like this before, and he sure wasn't looking like he was joking.

Rugs were turned over, drawers flung open, and tables were upside down. His employees wondered, "What's with this dollar. He has millions of it stashed in the bank, and the shoes on his feet are even worth thousands." Suddenly they heard an ecstatic voice from his office. "Yes, I found it!" The employees had to fake their excitement. One of them mustered the courage to ask the boss what was so special about this dollar, the rich man answered: "I may be rich, but a dollar is still a dollar, and it is mine."

THIS STORY IS ABOUT YOU.

There are over 7.3 billion people in the world today, and you may be wondering if God can see you or if He even knows your name.

Luke 12:7 says

"Indeed, the very hairs on your head are numbered..."

God loves and knows you, even before you were born

Jeremiah 1:5 says

"Before I formed you in your mother's womb, I knew you..."

and just like the rich man, God has gone above and beyond to make way for you to know Him.

Romans 5:8 says

"While we were yet sinners, Christ died for us"

You are too precious to God, and He wants to have a relationship with you.

You may be living in sin now; doing what you know in your heart is wrong, and, deep down you know that "This is NOT it" for you.

You know you were created for more than this.

There is hope and a way out for you.

HERE IS YOUR ESCAPE ROUTE

1. Acknowledge that you are a sinner

2. Romans 6:22, *"for everyone has sinned and have fallen short of God's standards..."*

3. Confess your sins to Jesus

4. 1st john 1:19 *"if we confess our sins to Him, He is faithful and just to forgive us and cleanse us from all unrighteousness..."*

5. Repent (a complete change of lifestyle)

6. Luke 13:3 *"repent or you will perish..."*

7. Confess that Jesus is your Lord (Lord means owner)

8. Romans 10:9, *"if you confess with your mouth that Jesus is Lord and that God raised Him from the dead, you will be saved."*

9. Let Jesus in

Revelation 3:20 "behold I stand at the door knocking, anyone who will hear and open I will come in and dine with him."

PRAY THIS

Lord Jesus, I know I am a sinner in need of you. Please forgive me for all my sins, wash me with your blood, give me a new heart with new desires too. I surrender to you now, be my Lord and make a way out of this mess for me. I pray in Jesus name, Amen.

If you've made it here, well, congratulations to you!!! The greatest miracle has just happened to you!

1/18/24

LET THE HEALING PROCESS BEGIN

Just because you ask Jesus into your life doesn't mean that you will suddenly forget your pain and like magic, it all disappears. No, it doesn't work that way, it is a process, but your healing can happen faster if you ALLOW God work on your mind and spirit. God respects our freewill and will never impose even the great Love He has for us.

We must willingly stretch forth our hands and receive the freedom He so lovingly offers. This will not be easy because He will require you to let go or do things you are totally uncomfortable with so that your freedom process can begin. There is a difference between holding the parachute before the jump and properly putting it on before the jump. Knowing about Jesus and LETTING Him take the wheels in your dark times are two different things, you must humble yourself and be ready to trust and obey.

 "Before any outside force can impact and influence, the inner force must first be surrendered" – Imaobong Smart

Healing begins from within you, this is always the first step before therapy and medicine.

The healing process will require you to be willing to open up to Him about your hurt. Sometimes it is hard to talk even to

God about the hurt you have experienced, but a sealed lip can sometimes be a chained life, when you talk about your hurt you gradually break the chains of depression one link at a time. God knows your pain, but He wants you to speak to Him about it, because in your speaking lies your freedom. Feel free to express yourself to Him, He is not holding a hammer to strike you when you express your anger and grievances to Him, He is OK with it.

"What a friend we have in Jesus, all our sins and grieves to bear,

what a privilege to carry everything to God in prayer, oh what peace we often forfeit and what needless pain we bear, all because we do not carry everything to God in prayer"- Joseph M Scriven

You must be transformed by the renewing of your mind, you renew your mind by letting go of what you now know and feel about your current state and learning to believe what God knows and says about you, and that can only be done by reading the Bible daily.

You must also be willing to carry out the very difficult task of FORGIVING anyone who hurt you deeply. This is NO JOKE, but it is POSSIBLE, and it is the KEY to your FREEDOM.

When you corporate with God in your healing process, the stronghold of depression and suicidal thoughts will be destroyed from your life.

Send me a personal message to staying4real@gmail.com and we will share your survival story.

01/19/24

References

https://www.who.int/mental_health/prevention/suicide/suicideprevent/en/

https://www.cdc.gov/violenceprevention/suicide/resources.html

https://www.cnbc.com/2018/02/22/medical-errors-third-leading-cause-of-death-in-america.html
https://www.hopkinsmedicine.org/news/media/releases/diagnostic_errors_more_common_costly_and_harmful_than_treatment_mistakes

https://www.sciencedaily.com/releases/2015/10/151022094959.htm

https://www.ncbi.nlm.nih.gov/pubmed/21234317

https://psychcentral.com/news/2011/08/10/bitterness-can-make-you-sick/28503.html

https://www.healthline.com/health-news/mental-listening-to-music-lifts-or-reinforces-mood-051713#2

https://www.wayoflife.org/reports/rock_music_and_suicide.html

https://biblehub.com/

https://biblehub.com/proverbs/12-25.htm

https://biblehub.com/genesis/1-27.htm

https://biblehub.com/jeremiah/1-5.htm

https://biblehub.com/luke/12-7.htm

https://biblehub.com/ecclesiastes/1-9.htm

https://biblehub.com/proverbs/14-12.htm

https://biblehub.com/1_corinthians/10-13.htm

https://biblehub.com/john/14-6.htm

https://biblehub.com/psalms/46-1.htm

https://biblehub.com/acts/2-21.htm

https://biblehub.com/isaiah/1-18.htm

https://biblehub.com/isaiah/1-18.htm

https://biblehub.com/isaiah/43-25.htm

https://biblehub.com/psalms/51-17.htm

https://biblehub.com/isaiah/55-7.htm

https://biblehub.com/1_samuel/2-9.htm

https://biblehub.com/matthew/11-28.htm

https://biblehub.com/1_peter/5-7.htm

https://biblehub.com/joel/3-10.htm

https://biblehub.com/isaiah/40-29.htm

https://biblehub.com/john/15-13.htm

https://biblehub.com/john/3-16.htm

https://biblehub.com/john/16-33.htm

https://biblehub.com/psalms/42-11.htm

https://biblehub.com/psalms/40-1.htm

https://biblehub.com/psalms/34-18.htm

https://biblehub.com/2_corinthians/10-5.htm

https://biblehub.com/proverbs/23-7.htm

https://biblehub.com/philippians/4-8.htm

https://biblehub.com/1_corinthians/6-15.htm

https://biblehub.com/proverbs/27-6.htm

https://biblehub.com/philippians/4-6.htm

https://biblehub.com/daniel/9-18.htm

https://biblehub.com/1_john/5-14.htm

https://biblehub.com/james/4-7.htm

Transformational speaker, author and purpose coach.

www.imaobongsmart.com

Visit my website and download my free eBook "what's your problem?" it's a purpose trigger questioner to help you discover the problems you were born to solve.

THANK YOU

Thank you for reading all the way to the end! If this book has helped you in any way at all, please share with your friends and help someone else STAY.

Don't forget to leave a review about this book, someone else could read and STAY because of it.

Use hashtag #Istayed!

Made in United States
Orlando, FL
01 September 2022

21850941R20061